IL POMO D'ORO
(Music from Acts III and V from Modena, Biblioteca Estense, Ms. Mus. E. 120)

RECENT RESEARCHES IN THE MUSIC OF THE BAROQUE ERA

Robert L. Marshall, general editor

A-R Editions, Inc., publishes six quarterly series—

Recent Researches in the Music of the Middle Ages and Early Renaissance,
Margaret Bent, general editor;

Recent Researches in the Music of the Renaissance,
James Haar and Howard Mayer Brown, general editors;

Recent Researches in the Music of the Baroque Era,
Robert L. Marshall, general editor;

Recent Researches in the Music of the Classical Era,
Eugene K. Wolf, general editor;

Recent Researches in the Music of the Nineteenth and Early Twentieth Centuries,
Rufus Hallmark, general editor;

Recent Researches in American Music,
H. Wiley Hitchcock, general editor—

which make public music that is being brought to light
in the course of current musicological research.

Each volume in the *Recent Researches* is devoted
to works by a single composer or to a single genre of composition,
chosen because of its potential interest to scholars and performers,
and prepared for publication according to the standards that govern
the making of all reliable historical editions.

Subscribers to this series, as well as patrons of subscribing institutions,
are invited to apply for information about the "Copyright-Sharing Policy"
of A-R Editions, Inc., under which the contents of this volume
may be reproduced free of charge for study or performance.

Correspondence should be addressed:

A-R EDITIONS, INC.
315 West Gorham Street
Madison, Wisconsin 53703

Antonio Cesti

IL POMO D'ORO

(Music for Acts III and V
from Modena, Biblioteca Estense, Ms. Mus. E. 120)

Edited by Carl B. Schmidt

A-R EDITIONS, INC. • MADISON

For Betsey

COPYRIGHT © 1982
A-R EDITIONS, INC.
ISSN 0484-0828
ISBN 0-89579-168-4

Library of Congress Cataloging in Publication Data:
Cesti, Antonio, 1623-1669.
   Il pomo d'oro. Music for Acts III and V from
Modena, Biblioteca Estense.

   (Recent researches in the music of the baroque era,
ISSN 0484-0828 ; v. 42)
   Reconstruction of portions of Acts 3 and 5 of the
opera from the ms. (Mus. E 120) which contains
excerpts from all acts with continuo acc.
   Libretto by Francesco Sbarra.
   Unfigured bass realized for keyboard instrument.
   Includes the texts for the lost portions of the work.
   Includes bibliographical references.
   1. Operas—Excerpts—Vocal scores with
continuo.   I. Schmidt, Carl B.   II. Sbarra,
Francesco, 17th cent.   III. Title.   IV. Series.
M2.R238   vol. 42   [M1508]   82-18419
ISBN 0-89579-168-4

Contents

IL POMO D'ORO

Atto Terzo

Preface

Introduction

> The Emperor, being in ecstasy,
> In order to receive with pomp,
> The illustrious object of his love,
> Has prepared everything in his court
> Because at last the Infanta from Spain
> Has, as we hear, begun her journey
> To come extinguish his fires.
> Oh! That they will both be happy,
> And that the Cupids, their accomplices,
> Will let them taste of delights
> After so many sighs
> And so many languishing desires![1]

These words, written by Charles Robinet on 15 May 1666, capture the impatience with which Emperor Leopold I awaited the arrival of his Spanish bride, Margarita, who had just embarked on the long voyage from Madrid to Vienna. The Emperor's impatience can clearly be traced to a series of premature deaths in the Austrian and Spanish lines of the Hapsburgs that left the succession squarely on the shoulders of Leopold, then twenty-six and still unmarried, and of Charles II, whose health was suspect.[2] While the Viennese court anxiously awaited the Infanta's arrival (delayed first by illness and then by travel problems), Leopold marshaled all the resources at his command to prepare a cornucopia of theatrical entertainments in her honor. Some of the more modest of these events were performed during the fall of 1666 to occupy the court while it waited, but lavish festivities were reserved until after Margarita's formal entry into Vienna in December of 1666. Though Leopold apparently left the creators of the lesser entertainments to their own devices, he was personally involved with two grand enterprises, Antonio Bertali's and Johann Heinrich Schmelzer's *balletto* titled *La contesa dell'aria e dell'acqua* and Antonio Cesti's opera *Il pomo d'oro*. That Leopold attended rehearsals of the *balletto* is manifest from his own letters. Moreover, in addition to following the progress of the preparation of the opera, Leopold actually composed some of its music (see below).[3] The size and number of theatrical performances honoring Leopold's first marriage must have created a severe drain on both the human and financial resources of the court; the nature of these performances has been fully documented in an article by Herbert Seifert.[4] Here, however, we focus our attention solely on the opera *Il*

pomo d'oro, a work that history has accorded a lofty position among the most magnificent baroque entertainments ever staged.

The libretto of *Il pomo d'oro* was commissioned by Leopold I from Francesco Sbarra. Antonio Cesti (who had recently been brought by Leopold to Vienna from Innsbruck) was assigned to compose the music.[5] Since composer and librettist had collaborated before (e.g., on *Alessandro vincitor di se stesso* [Venice, 1651], on *La magnanimità d'Alessardro* [Innsbruck, 1662], and on *Nettuno e flora festeggianti* [Vienna, July 1666]), one assumes that they were able to move ahead on *Il pomo d'oro* with some dispatch. Apparently Leopold's commission was given early in 1666, because Cesti was already busy composing on 27 June of that year. Composition was continued throughout the summer (music for the Prologue and half of Act I was finished by 8 August), but the bulk of the music was probably not completed before late fall of 1666.[6] Strong evidence suggests that Leopold intended to have the opera performed as soon as all the necessary preparations could be completed; however, equally strong evidence indicates that projected performances during late 1666, 1667, and early 1668 failed to materialize.[7] Among the contributing factors to this apparent failure were the delayed arrival of the future Empress (late in 1666) and the unfinished state of a new theater that was being built to accommodate the production. Moreover, even after Margarita arrived, the performance of *Il pomo d'oro* was probably further delayed by the mourning period following the death, after only a few months of life, of the royal couple's first-born son. Performance was finally achieved on the occasion of Margarita's birthday in July of 1668. Because the opera contained a prologue plus five acts and numerous ballets that took many hours to perform, it was decided to present the 1668 performance over the course of two days, with the prologue and first two acts premiering on 12 July, and Acts III, IV, and V being performed on 14 July.[8] Contemporary accounts praised this performance, and the libretto was published in Spanish (Vienna, 1668) and German (Nuremberg, 1672).[9] A German synopsis was also printed in Vienna during 1668.

It is often forgotten that in spite of its historical prominence, none of the music of *Il pomo d'oro* was published at the time of the initial performance of the opera. Moreover, although modern scholarship has provided an edition of the heretofore extant music (i.e., the Prologue and Acts I, II, and IV, contained in a manuscript held by the Österreichische Nationalbibliothek in Vienna),[10] and although several seventeenth-century prints of the libretto include engravings that show the magnificence of the sets for this opera, some of the many problems connected with this work have only recently been considered. For example, the year of first performance of *Il pomo d'oro* has been listed as, alternatively, 1666, 1667, or 1668 (see above); until recently, the literary sources for the libretto have not been thoroughly studied, and music for two of the five acts (Act III and Act V) has been missing. Fortunately, a manuscript in the Biblioteca Estense in Modena—Ms. Mus. E. 120—has now been located that contains excerpts from all of the opera except the Prologue. Although in the Modena manuscript Cesti's rich instrumentation has been reduced to continuo and an occasional rubric that indicates which instruments should be present, we are now able to restore portions of the missing two acts. This edition presents the reconstruction of Acts III and V made possible by the discovery of material from the Modena manuscript. In order to make this reconstruction as useful as possible, the complete text for Acts III and V has been included here with the music interpolated from the Modena manuscript. Sometimes only isolated arias exist in the Modena manuscript, but in several instances whole scenes are given. No attempt has been made to reconstruct missing *ritornelli* or instrumental accompaniments for Acts III and V; this task would be fruitful only if the Modena manuscript contained far more of the missing music than it actually does. The purpose of this edition is to add to our understanding of *Il pomo d'oro* and to further our growing knowledge of Antonio Cesti as an important figure in the history of seventeenth-century Italian opera.

The Sources

The sole source for the music in this edition is Modena, Biblioteca Estense, Ms. Mus. E. 120 (designated in the Critical Notes as I: MOe), which contains excerpts from all five acts of *Il pomo d'oro* as follows: Act I (14 numbers); Act II (9 numbers); Act III (9 numbers); Act IV (10 numbers); and Act V (8 numbers). As used in this Preface, the word "number" refers to a block of contiguous music in a scene that occurs before an omission of text in the source. Only the selections from Acts III and V of the Modena source are included in this edition, since the Prologue and Acts I, II, and IV have already appeared in Guido Adler's edition of Vienna, Österreichische Nationalbibliothek Ms. 16885.[11]

The Modena manuscript is comprised of seventy-six numbered folios, plus unnumbered folios at the beginning and end. A modern inventory of the contents appears on the first unnumbered folio (recto and verso) under the rubric "Scene diverse Con Musica di S[u]a M[aes]tà Cesarea." When the Modena manuscript is compared with the extant libretti, we can see that this Modena source presents the musical numbers in strict order of acts and scenes.[12] Four of the numbers ("Su l'età," "Anderò," and "Ah quest è vero," from Act II, and "Amante disprezzata" from Act V) are attributed to Leopold I in the Modena source, and the remainder are unascribed. Thus, until recently, it had been thought that Leopold was the composer of all of the works in Ms. Mus. E. 120. However, of the unascribed pieces in the Modena manuscript that correspond to the texts from Acts I, II, and IV of *Il pomo d'oro*, all are concordant with what we know to be Cesti's music in the Österreichische Nationalbibliothek source. Therefore, there is little doubt that even though the unascribed numbers from Acts III and V are unique to the Modena source, Cesti is the composer of this music also.

Since the Modena manuscript contains only portions of the music for Acts III and V, text linking these sections of music within each act has been supplied for this edition from the libretto (large format edition), printed in Vienna in 1668.[13] Stage directions given in square brackets ([ ]) have also been taken from the 1668 libretto. The specific exemplar used here is from Bologna, Biblioteca Universitaria, A.M.TT.II.14.

Editorial Practice

The note values, time signatures, and key signatures of the source have been retained throughout the edition. The music accompanying the first appearance of each dramatic character is preceded by an indication of the original clef; in this edition, all clef signs have been regularized to treble or bass clefs. Accidentals have been preserved as in the source, except in the case of a redundant appearance of the same inflection within a measure. Editorial accidentals have been placed in brackets on the staff, and a natural sign has replaced a sharp or flat when these signs are used in the source to cancel one another. Editorial accidentals that caution against inflection are enclosed in parentheses.

The source gives the solo line and an accompanying bass line (see Plates I and II). The few bass figures that appear in the Modena manuscript are retained in this edition (with 6♯ regularized to ♯6), and editorial bass figures are added only at certain cadences to suggest bass figures given by the source for earlier statements of the same music. The realization (given here in cue-sized notation) is editorial.

Original barlines have been kept except in rare instances: in such instances, the original placement of the barlines is indicated in this edition by a vertical slash touching the top of a stave (e.g., on p. 26, mm. 19-21). All editorial barlines, necessitated primarily in $\frac{3}{2}$ sections, appear as broken lines. Editorial phrase marks, enclosed in brackets in this edition, have been added only for the sake of consistency within a given aria. In other matters, such as the reduction of two tied half-notes to a whole-note (occasioned by a measure that is divided over two systems in the source), modern editorial procedures have been tacitly followed.

The underlaid text of this edition has been modernized in terms of spelling and punctuation; the phonetics and syntax of the source have not been altered. The use of the Italian accents in the text conforms to the conventions established in *Vocabolario della lingua italiana*.[14] For the underlaid text, the versification has been editorially indicated through the use of capital letters at the beginning of each new verse line; *ij* passages have been written out and enclosed within angled brackets (< >). All editorial additions of text or of stage directions that are given in the course of the musical numbers are taken from the 1668 Vienna libretto; all such additions are enclosed in square brackets.

Performance Practice

The bass of this edition has been realized for a keyboard instrument in order to facilitate performance for those whose experience is insufficient to allow improvisation from bass figures. The realization has been kept relatively simple except in those few places where the singer rests for several measures. There has been no attempt to maintain strict contrapuntal voice leading in realizing the bass. Because the manuscript is only sparsely figured, there are many occasions where more than one chord solution is possible. This is particularly true at cadences where suspensions and sevenths can easily be added *ad libitum*. The editor hopes that anyone who is interested and able will follow the common baroque practice of creating his own realization. No dynamic marks appear in the Modena manuscript, and the editor has chosen not to add any here.

Critical Notes

In the notes that follow, the unicum Modena manuscript is cited as I:MOe, and the 1668 Vienna printed libretto is referred to as "1668." The first verse line of underlaid text of each number provides the title citation for each entry. Pitches are given according to the Helmholtz system, wherein c' = middle C, c'' = the c above middle C, and so forth.

Atto Terzo

SCENA PRIMA

"Ha la forza dell'oro ogni virtù"—M. 10, one line of text found at this point in 1668 (*E che vuoi di più?*) has not been set to music in I:MOe. Mm. 49-55, in I:MOe the text for strophe 2 is both underlaid and given in paragraph form at the conclusion of the aria, while the

text for strophe 3 is given only in paragraph form at the conclusion of the aria.

"Ed io Zeffiro con Flora"—In I:MOe, the text for strophe 3 is given only in paragraph form at the conclusion of the aria.

[SCENA TERZA]

"Ahi lassa, dov'è"—M. 2, basso continuo, I:MOe gives bass figures here, but they are illegible. Mm. 1-8, underlaid text is *Ahi dove dov'è* in I:MOe.

SCENA QUARTA

"Ennone dispietata"—M. 24, 1668 gives this text as *trovi fra poco*. M. 30, basso continuo, I:MOe gives figures $^6_4{}^\sharp$ for note 2.

SCENA QUINTA

"L'esser vivo a quanto giova!"—Mm. 16-76, 1668 reverses the order of strophes 2 and 3. M. 21, basso continuo, note 1 is e in I:MOe. M. 30, basso continuo, notes 2-5 are B c d e in I:MOe. M. 47, voice and basso continuo, the meter signature "3" occurs in I:MOe. M. 76, basso continuo, note 1 is a quarter in I:MOe.

SCENA SESTA

"Ei, forse sarà"—Mm. 40-42, underlaid text is *Non è la mia fiamma* in I:MOe.

"Troppo Pallade pretende"—M. 19, basso continuo, note 6 is e in I:MOe.

SCENA DECIMA

"Quand'Ennone ancora"—M. 37, Filaura, notes 1 and 2 are eighth-notes in I:MOe. M. 135, in place of the text *Quei sospiri*, I:MOe gives the sign ⸙ and then erroneously repeats the word "sospiri." M. 140, Filaura, note 3, flat placed after rather than before the note in I:MOe. M. 142, basso continuo, note 2 is e-flat in I:MOe. M. 163, Filaura, note 3 is e'' in the analogous passage at m. 128.

[Atto Quinto]

SCENA SECONDA

"Imparate in avvenire"—M. 11, Ennone, rhythm of this m. is dotted half, three quarters, in I:MOe. M. 17, Ennone, note 2 is sharped in I:MOe. M. 57, Ennone, note 4 is flatted in I:MOe.

SCENA TERZA

"Che mi val aver fratello"—M. 8, basso continuo, note 4 is F in I:MOe.

"Guidicar retto e sincero"—Mm. 1-38, text for strophe 2 is given only in paragraph form at the conclusion of the aria in I:MOe. Mm. 44 ff., the indication *Se ne va* is lacking in I:MOe and 1668. Mm. 61-62, text is *D'un fosco velo* in 1668.

[SCENA QUARTA]

"Olà, diva che fai?"—M. 11, Giunone, text underlaid to note 3 is *i* instead of *nei* in 1668. M. 27, voice and basso continuo, the meter signature "3" occurs in I:MOe. Mm. 29 (last note)-33 (note 2), underlaid text is *S'accenda la terra* in I:MOe. M. 37, Giunone, notes 2 and 3 are g' and c'' in I:MOe. Mm. 51-52, order of text is reversed to *orrido Ed torrido* in I:MOe. M. 76, voice and basso continuo, the meter signature "C" occurs in I:MOe. M. 77, Momo, sharp appears between notes 5 and 6 in I:MOe. M. 88, Momo, note 16 is a in I:MOe. M. 155, basso continuo, note 4 is f in I:MOe. M. 166, basso continuo, figured bass symbol 6♯ is given below note 3 in I:MOe.

[SCENA QUINTA]

"Amante disprezzata"—M. 12, basso continuo, note 3 is A in I:MOe. M. 36, Ennone, note 1 is a' in I:MOe. M. 81, basso continuo, bass figures 4-3 given for strophe 1 by I:MOe.

SCENA SETTIMA

"Lascia andar chi se ne va"—Mm. 1-2, 1668 gives *Or pensar non più si de* for this text. M. 20, the indication "Segue Aurindo" has been added in I:MOe by a mod-ern hand. M. 25, Aurindo, note 4 is a quarter-note in I:MOe. M. 29, Aurindo, note 1 is d in I:MOe. Mm. 43-47, all voice parts, underlaid text is *Fedele, Costante* in 1668.

Acknowledgments

The author wishes to thank the administration of the Modena, Biblioteca Estense for providing the film of the source on which this edition is based. Thanks are also due the administration of the Biblioteca Universitaria in Bologna for providing access to the 1668 printed edition of the libretto by Francesco Sbarra. A special debt of gratitude is owed to Lorenzo Bianconi of the University of Arezzo for having edited the Italian text and for having made many valuable suggestions.

Carl B. Schmidt
Philadelphia College of the
Performing Arts

June 1982

Notes

1. L'EMPEREUR, étant en Extase
Pour recevoir avec emphase
L['] illustre OBJET de son Amour,
Fait tout préparer dans sa COUR,
Car enfin l'INFANTE d'ESPAGNE
S'est, ce dit-on, mise en campagne
Pour venir appaiser ses feux.
Ah! qu'ils seront aises tous deux
Et que les Amours, leurs Complices,
Leur feront goûter de délices
Aprés tant & tant de soûpirs
Et tant de languissans désirs!

See James de Rothschild, ed., *Les Continuateurs de Loret: Lettres en vers de La Gravette de Mayolas, Robinet, Boursault, Perdou de Subligny, Laurent et autres (1665-1689)*, 3 vols. (Paris: Damascène Morgand and Charles Fatout, 1881), I: col. 866. Many other valuable references to Margarita's journey and her years in Vienna are contained in Rothschild's edition.

2. John P. Spielman, *Leopold I of Austria* (New Brunswick, New Jersey: Rutgers University Press, 1977), pp. 46-47.

3. For a documentary survey of the problems surrounding the composer attribution and the performance of *Il pomo d'oro*, see Carl B. Schmidt, "Antonio Cesti's *Il pomo d'oro*: A Reexamination of a Famous Hapsburg Court Spectacle," *Journal of the American Musicological Society* 29 (1976): 381-412. Many of the details given in that article have not been repeated here.

4. See Herbert Seifert, "Die Festlichkeiten zur ersten Hochzeit Kaiser Leopolds I.," *Österreichische Musikzeitschrift* 29 (1974): 6-16. I am extremely grateful to Dr. Seifert for his generosity in sharing additional information that either confirms or corrects details in the article listed in note 3.

5. Detailed biographical information concerning Antonio Cesti is available in *The New Grove Dictionary of Music and Musicians*, s.v. "Antonio Cesti," by David Burrows and Carl B. Schmidt, and in the *Dizionario biografico degli italiani*, s.v. "Antonio Cesti," by Lorenzo Bianconi.

6. See Remo Giazotto, "Nel CCC anno della morte di Antonio Cesti: Ventidue lettere ritrovate nell'Archivio di Stato di Venezia," *Nuova rivista musicale italiana* III (1969): 510, and Carl B. Schmidt, "The Operas of Antonio Cesti" (Ph. D. diss., Harvard University, 1973), I: App. I, p. 108.

7. This evidence is summarized in Schmidt, "Antonio Cesti's *Il pomo d'oro*," pp. 384-390.

8. To the documentation listed in Schmidt, "Antonio Cesti's *Il pomo d'oro*" can be added the following significant points that have kindly been communicated to me by letter (13 July 1977) from Dr. Seifert. First, a letter from Count Paul Esterházy to his brother, dated 21 December 1667, reported from Eisenstadt that *Il pomo d'oro* was to be presented after the feast days. On 2 January, however, a second letter, written in answer to his brother's query, stated that although no performance had yet taken place, Count Paul thought one would take place within a few days. Second, a letter from Count Esterházy to his wife on 13 July 1668 stated that half of the comedy had been performed the day before (12 July), and that the remaining half would be performed on Saturday, 14 July. This information emends the date given in Schmidt, "Antonio Cesti's *Il pomo d'oro*." For the original Hungarian quotations, see Johann Harich, *Burgendländische Forschungen . . . Festgabe anlässlich der 150. Wiederkehr des Todestages von Joseph Haydn*, Esterházy-Musikgeschichte im Spiegel der zeitgenössischen Textbücher, 39 (Eisenstadt, 1959), pp. 5-6.

9. Two other literary sources of the libretto may be added to those listed in Schmidt, "Antonio Cesti's *Il pomo d'oro*": (1) a manuscript libretto in German translation, now in the Coburg, Landesbibliothek (MS 104), listed by Ilona Hubay, *Die Handschriften der Landesbibliothek Coburg* (Coburg: Coburger Landesstiftung, 1962); and (2) a Spanish translation (mentioned to me by Dr. Seifert in his letter of 13 July 1977) by Juan Silvestre Salvo (or Salva) published in Vienna during 1668 and titled *La manzana de oro*. The Spanish translation is cited by D. Cayetano Alberto de la Barrera y Leirado in his *Catálogo bibliográfico y biográfico del teatro antiquo español* (Madrid, 1860), p. 362. Copies of this libretto can be found in the Madrid, Biblioteca Nacional, Sección de Raros (R-19783 and R-1690-10). Salvo also translated Minato's libretto titled *La prosperità d'Elio Sejano*, which was first performed with Antonio Sartorio's music in Venice during 1667. A copy of his translation, published in 1671, may be found in the British Library (11726.a.15.[1]).

10. Guido Adler's edition of the Prologue and Acts I, II, and IV is published in *Denkmäler der Tonkunst in Österreich*, Jg. III/2 (Bd. 6) and Jg. IV/2 (Bd. 9) (Vienna: Breitkopf & Härtel, 1896-97; reprint ed., Graz: Akademische Druck u. Verlagsanstalt, 1959). Adler's edition has as its source the set of volumes once owned by Leopold I and now held by the Österreichische Nationalbibliothek (Ms. 16885). Adler gives only text for Acts III and V in his edition.

11. Ibid.

12. For more detailed information on the Modena manuscript, see Schmidt, "Antonio Cesti's *Il pomo d'oro*," Appendix B.

13. Two Italian editions of this libretto were printed in 1668: one in large format containing engravings of set designs, the other in small format and lacking such engravings.

14. Nicola Zingarelli, *Vocabolario della lingua italiana*, 10th ed. (1970).

Appendix

The Plot

In order to provide continuity between the text of this edition of Acts III and V and that in the edition by Guido Adler of the Prologue and Acts I, II, and IV, a brief plot summary of the entire opera is presented here. Egon Wellesz has already published a discussion of the plot involved in those parts of *Il pomo d'oro* edited by Adler, but no English language summary of the action that occurs in Acts III and V has been available.[1] The libretto of *Il pomo d'oro* is far too long to translate here; the following synopsis is intended to provide an overview of the plot and its manifold intricacies.

At a time when such librettists as Aurelio Aureli and Nicolò Minato chose to write libretti that (except in their prologues) make no reference to the Greek gods, Francesco Sbarra returned to the classic Greek myth commonly known as "The Judgment of Paris" for the basic scenario of his *Il pomo d'oro*.[2] In Sbarra's recounting, the basic story is embellished with newly contrived sub-plots and with the addition of three new major characters: Momo (a sort of court jester); Filaura (a sympathetic nurse of the type well known from other Venetian libretti); and Aurindo (a shepherd in love with Ennone). This expansion resulted in a libretto that sprawled over a prologue and five acts at a time when most operas were only three acts long. As noted above, *Il pomo d'oro* was so long that it took two days to perform, and Sbarra spared no expense as he called for one of the largest, most diverse casts ever assembled on the seventeenth-century operatic stage.

The Prologue

The Prologue of *Il pomo d'oro* is among the longest and most demanding to grace the operatic stage before the advent of Jean-Baptiste Lully's *tragédies lyriques* (first performed in France in the early 1670s). This opening section is devoted to a statement of the glory of Austria as reflected by the benevolent monarch Leopold I. Such encomiastic prologues, typical of Hapsburg court entertainments, were frequently paired with a *licenza* (a dedication) at the end of the opera, and Sbarra's libretto for *Il pomo d'oro* follows this plan. In the Prologue of *Il pomo d'oro*, Sbarra used personifications of the provinces and kingdoms that constituted the Austrian Empire in order to pay homage to Leopold: among those chosen were Hungary, Italy, Bohemia, Spain, Austria, America (a bit of presumption), and Sardinia. The stage setting for the Prologue is opulent. The print showing Ludovico Burnacini's décor depicts an ornately decorated hall of pillars. Alternating with the pillars are niches, each of which contains one of twelve equestrian statues of former Austrian rulers. The rows of pillars converge at the rear of the stage, where Emperor Leopold is depicted astride a spirited mount supported by the captured spoils of war. Above them all, a character called La Gloria Austriaca (The Glory of Austria) can be seen mounted on the mythological horse Pegasus.

Act I

In Act I, Sbarra's libretto establishes the basic outline of the plot as given in the traditional myth. According to Greek mythology, Discord (Discordia), having been excluded from the Olympian nuptials of Thetis and Peleus, was sent back by Pluto to Mt. Olympus to throw a golden apple inscribed "For the most beautiful" amidst the assembled wedding guests. This deed caused an exceedingly quarrelsome debate among the goddesses Juno (Giunone), Athena (Pallas), and Venus (Venere), each of whom had risen to claim the prize. Jupiter (Giove), as king of the gods, was then obliged to settle the matter by submitting the three claims to a mortal for judgment. He nominated Paris (Paride), son of King Priam of Troy, to hear arguments from each goddess in turn. Jupiter's envoy Mercury (Mercurio) then led the three goddesses to Phrygia, where Paris was guarding his father's sheep on Mt. Ida. Paris was more than reluctant to fulfill Jupiter's command, but he could not refuse such a high authority. Subsequently, each of the three goddesses offered Paris a reward to make his judgment in her favor. Juno promised to make Paris lord over all Asia (Sbarra included Europe as well), Athena promised to make Paris eternally victorious in battle, and Venus, using her womanly guile, simply disrobed and promised to give Paris his choice of the most beautiful of mortal women. Euripides recounts the event in somewhat more poetic terms in his play *Trojan Women*:

> And this Paris judged beneath the trees
> Three Crowns of Life, three diverse Goddesses.
> The gift of Pallas was of War, to lead
> His East in conquering battles, and make bleed
> The hearths of Hellas. Hera held a Throne—
> If majesties he craved—to reign alone
> From Phrygia to the last realm of the West.
> And Cypris, if he deemed her loveliest,
> Beyond all heaven, made dreams about my face

And for her grace gave me [i.e., Helen]. And, lo! her
  grace
Was judged the fairest, and she stood above
Those twain.[3]

Sbarra's libretto is faithful to this basic plot outline, but he embellished it considerably. His opening scenes are set in Pluto's (Plutone's) realm, where Persephone (Proserpina) and the lord of the underworld (seated on thrones and attended by various demons and infernal monsters) are engaged in a discussion (scenes 1-3).[4] Persephone complains bitterly that her lot is to live in darkness, and Pluto is unable to console her. They are joined by Discord, who is riding a fire-breathing dragon and who is intent on creating some sort of dissension among the gods. At Pluto's command, Discord rides off to initiate the argument over the golden apple. As the scene changes to the palace of Jupiter on Mt. Olympus, the banquet is in full swing, and various gods, including Apollo, Mars (Marte), Neptune (Nettuno), Bacchus (Bacco), and Mercury, all drink and offer brief speeches (scene 4). Sbarra injected some humor at this point by including a *buffone*, named Momo, who is prominent throughout the opera, and who makes humorous remarks here at the expense of Mars. This festive scene also includes the three principal goddesses, as well as Hebe, Ganymede, and a chorus of lesser gods, whose function it is to wait on table. After much merrymaking, Discord arrives to cast the golden apple, and, except for Momo, who is finally left alone to comment on the role Paris will soon play, events follow the Greek myth (scene 5).

The action now shifts to Mt. Ida, where Sbarra fleshes out the myth by introducing the lovely nymph Ennone (daughter of Xanthus, river god of the Scamander in ancient Troas), who is in love with Paris (scene 6).[5] Ennone is soon joined by Paris, and a love duet follows that heightens the anticipation of the "Judgment" (scene 7). That a portion of this duet is overheard by Aurindo, a shepherd who is in love with Ennone, provides fuel for later turns of the sub-plots. The amorous scene between Paris and Ennone is interrupted by Mercury's cloud-borne arrival. To Ennone's dismay, Mercury announces the role that Paris must soon play (scene 8). In scene 9, Aurindo laments constantly about his unrequited love for Ennone, and in scene 10, Filaura (Ennone's nurse) listens with mock sympathy to Aurindo's description of his plight. The first act ends with Juno and Athena presenting themselves (after having made spectacular flying entrances) to Paris in his palace courtyard. They each offer him what amounts to a bribe (scenes 11-14). Momo, himself making an impressive airborne entrance supported by several cupids, enlivens these scenes with countless urgings and suggestions to Paris. For Venus's offer to Paris (see above), the scene is changed to a pleasure garden replete with a cast of supernu-

meraries (scene 15). As the dramatic action of Act I concludes, Venus, having won the golden apple by promising to reward Paris with Helen, exults in her victory. The act ends with a ballet.

Act II

A unifying thread running throughout the remaining four acts of the opera is the retribution against Venus plotted and carried out by the defeated Juno and Athena. The first half of Act II concerns Paris's departure by ship to claim Helen. In the opening five scenes, Aurindo and Filaura continue to discuss his hopeless infatuation with Ennone. Aurindo implores Filaura for help in the match and obtains her promise of aid (scene 1). Once Aurindo has departed, Momo addresses Filaura, who listens willingly, and tells her about Paris's desire for Helen. His comments are, actually, more social comment than fact (scene 2). This opening pair of scenes is followed by a second pair in which Paris, alone, rhapsodizes about his new love (scene 3) and is then accused by Ennone and Filaura of breach of trust (scene 4). Paris denies their accusations and reaffirms his love for Ennone (see Act I, scene 7). The first half of Act II ends with scene 5, a solo scene in which Momo complains about the world in general and about Jupiter in particular.

The events leading up to Paris's departure are even further prolonged by a dramatic scene change. In scenes 6 and 7, the mouth of hell yawns open revealing Charon (Caronte), who is disconsolate over the lack of people to transport to the underworld. Three flying furies—Megaera (Megera), Alecto (Aletto), and Tesiphone (Tesifone)—enter and try to convince Charon to transport them across the River Styx. He agrees when they promise to reward him with a tale, and they tell him about a conflict involving goddesses that has shaken the world. It is about this conflict that they seek counsel in the underworld. Upon their departure, Charon exults that earthly strife will lead to increased power for his dominion. When the brief intermezzo occasioned by this digression is completed, the set reverts to the departure scene, and Paris is finally sent on his way with Venus and Cupid (Amore), who fly overhead (scenes 8 and 9).

The action shifts to an Athenian war camp, where Adraste (a priest), Cecrope (King of Athens), and soldiers are gathered (scene 10). Cecrope is joined first by Athena (scene 11), who informs him that Paris's choice has offended her and that Cecrope must take arms to defend her, and then by Alceste (his wife), who laments their frequent separation caused by wars (scene 12). After a show of affection between Cecrope and Alceste, Cecrope agrees to permit Alceste to accompany him on his next foray into battle. The scene then shifts for the fourth time in this act to a marsh representing Athena's birthplace. Having asked her friend King Cecrope to attack Paris for not having awarded her the golden apple, Athena departs, and the last two scenes (scenes 13 and 14) conclude with the arming and mock combat of Cecrope's troops. The act closes with the fully armed Athena standing on a cloud and demanding that Paris's affront to her be avenged.

Act III

Act III, the first for which music is printed in the present edition, begins (scene 1) in the cavern of the wind god Aeolus (Aeolo), who is attended by various other wind gods (e.g., the Sylvan god Zephyrus [Zeffiro] and his brother Eurus [Euro]). Their peaceful discussions (during which the Winds inform Aeolus of their various duties) are disturbed by the arrival of Juno on her cloud, who, following Athena's lead, rages against Paris and calls him a vile shepherd (scene 2). She suggests that Aeolus loose a fierce tempest to destroy Paris's ship.

At this point, three characters last seen at the beginning of Act II return. In scenes 3-5, set in the valley of the Xanthus river, Ennone, disconsolate at not being able to locate Paris, is joined by Aurindo and Momo. Although Ennone contemplates drowning herself, she is saved by Momo, who tells her that Paris is gone forever. This gives Aurindo hope for a future with Ennone as scene 5 concludes. However, this respite from martial events is brief; the scene quickly changes to Mars's arsenal (scene 6), where Venus, in her attempt to prove that Paris's judgment is fair, solicits Mars's assistance against the Athenian forces. Here, at the mid-point of the opera, the emphasis of the plot turns to development of the action that results from the vendetta between Venus and her two powerful rivals—Juno and Athena.

Having begun Act III with Juno invoking the assistance of Aeolus, Sbarra's libretto now returns to the matter of Paris's voyage. Aeolus throws his full fury at Paris and his ship (scene 7). Venus intercedes, however, and promises to give Neptune the nymph Amphitrite (Anfitrite) if he will calm the sea (scene 8). Neptune and his retinue rise from the sea and quickly calm it, Venus departs, and Paris is able to resume his voyage in search of Helen. Meanwhile Filaura and Aurindo are still unable to determine the whereabouts of Paris (scenes 9 and 10). The final scenes (11 and 12) of Act III are set in an amphitheater to which Cecrope and his soldiers have come to confront Mars and his warriors. When the fighting subsides, Mars is victorious and takes Cecrope prisoner.

Act IV

As Act IV begins (it is set in a cedar forest), the physical strife of the previous act is exchanged for the emo-tional turmoil of Ennone, who, once again, pours out her unhappiness at the still fruitless quest for Paris. Her complaint is heard by Filaura (scene 2) before the action reverts to more serious matters. A sufficient amount of time having elapsed since the staging of the previous natural phenomenon (the near shipwreck of Paris), the groundwork for a new catastrophe is laid in the next scene. The setting is the Temple of Athena in Athens, where the priest Adraste and assorted ministers are gathered for a solemn sacrificial ceremony (scene 3). Their invocations are answered by a terrible earthquake that causes the temple columns to crumble and the edifice to collapse. Athena then appears on a cloud and furiously informs the assembled worshippers that their king (Cecrope) has been taken prisoner and is in Mars's fortress along with the coveted golden apple (scene 4). Mars is now the subject of Athena's wrath. Adraste calls the assembled Athenians to arms, and they depart. Alceste overhears the proceedings and is thrilled to learn that her husband is still alive (scene 5).

The next group of scenes is unified by the element of fire. Fire first appears as a blazing circle around the Milky Way and finally is personified as L' Elemento del Foco (scenes 6-9). For the first time since Act I, Venus and Juno confront each other; and when they part, Venus heightens Juno's ire by reminding her that Mars possesses the golden apple. Juno then asks Fire (Foco) to destroy Neptune's realm as a punishment for Neptune's intervention in the sinking of Paris's ship. Fire rejects this request, saying it is forbidden by fate. Insulted, Juno departs, but Fire has the last word as the scene concludes.

Three secondary characters—the Graces Euphrosyne (Eufrosine), Aglaia (Aglaie), and Thalia (Pasithea)—are now seen in the entrance of the palace of Venus (scenes 10 and 11). Ironically, Euphrosyne, the personification of grace, arrives on the back of a tortoise (an awkward entrance at best), and can only lament her unfortunate lot. Their calm discussions, however, are interrupted by the arrival of Venus and Mars on a triumphal machine drawn by two lions ridden by Amorini (scene 12). In chains at their feet lies King Cecrope, and they are surrounded by the spoils of war that have been plundered from Juno and Athena. Over the head of Mars a triumphal crown can be seen, and over the head of Venus is the golden apple. An argument ensues in which Mars and Venus call Cecrope a slave while he, in turn, retorts that he is a king. Finally, Venus warns Cecrope that his tongue is also a prisoner and therefore he should keep silent! Their confrontation is interrupted by Cupid, who warns Mars and Venus that this is no time to exult, since the entire populace of Athens, aroused by Athena, is at their doorstep. Venus and Mars exhort all present to take arms (scene 13), and Cupid's story is quickly borne out as Adraste, accompanied by his army and Alceste (scene 14), approaches the fortress and begins a siege that involves two elephants mounted with platforms, ladders, and other paraphernalia. Athena, as usual, oversees the battle from her lofty position in the sky and intervenes to give the Athenians the advantage (scene 15).

Act V

As Act V begins, it is clear that no resolutions to the multifarious threads of the plot are in sight: the rival goddesses are still warring; Ennone has not yet located Paris; Paris has not found Helen; and numerous lesser gods are disconsolate. The complications are too much for anyone but the king of the gods to resolve, so, after two brief scenes (1-2, set in Paris's sumptuous palace) that involve Ennone, Filaura, and Momo, Jupiter, who has been absent since Act I (scene 3), reappears. Jupiter is immediately confronted by Juno, who expresses her anger that Jupiter presumed to have her judged by a mere mortal, even if this mortal was the most handsome man alive. In one of the opera's more dramatic moments, Juno unleashes a terrific thunderstorm, accompanied by rain, hail, thunder, and lightning, and she manages to terrify Momo, who had initially scoffed at her part in the vendetta (scene 4). The action then returns to Aurindo, who is heartsick to the point of suicide over Ennone's continued rejection of his affection (scenes 5-6). At the prodding of Filaura and Momo, however, Ennone finally abandons her search for Paris and submits to Aurindo (scenes 7-8). With the denouement now in full swing, the scene changes to a square in Mars's palace, where Jupiter is shown seated on a heavenly throne (scene 9). A ruined tower (containing the golden apple) is visible in the middle of the square, and Jupiter is attended by an eagle at his feet. Juno and Athena renew their bickering and so anger Jupiter that he asserts his authority by causing the tower to crumble and sends his eagle into the ruins to reclaim the golden apple.

As the final scene begins, Jupiter announces that he has found a way to satisfy each goddess (scene 10). At this point Sbarra's text deviates from the original mythological plot to return to pay homage to Leopold and Margarita. Jupiter's solution to the problem of the golden apple is to bestow the prize on Empress Margarita. As he does this, he says that she alone combines the greatness of Juno, the wisdom of Athena, and the beauty of Venus. A concealed room is then revealed in the loftiest heavenly position. This room contains the likenesses of Leopold, Margarita, and numerous progeny (in a bit of wishful thinking). All present then sing praises to the royal family, and the opera ends with not one, but three ballets: one for the spirits in the air; a second for knights on the earth; and a third for sirens and tritons in the sea.

Sbarra's conclusion, a brilliant and original concept, was clearly occasioned by the function of *Il pomo d'oro* as a wedding gift to Empress Margarita. Apparently Sbarra was not bothered by the facts that the ending is contrived, that most of the events after Act I are mere elaborations on the myth, and that there are many loose ends in this plot.[6] Sbarra's libretto remains a monument to the mid-seventeenth-century technique of building a lengthy text out of a relatively brief myth or historical account. Circumstances permitted Sbarra lavish means, both in terms of magnificent sets and extraordinary numbers of singers and supernumeraries. What the libretto lacks in cohesion is more than compensated for by the element of spectacle.

Notes to the Appendix

1. See Egon Wellesz, "Ein Bühnenfestspiel aus dem Siebzehnten Jahrhundert," *Die Musik* LII (1914): 191-217. This essay has been reissued in *Essays on Opera*, trans. Patricia Kean (London: Dennis Dobson, 1950), pp. 54-81.

2. A concise account of this myth, as well as references to its occurrence in classical literature, can be found in H. J. Rose, *A Handbook of Greek Mythology Including its Extension to Rome* (New York: E. P. Dutton, 1959), pp. 2 and 106. Precisely what occasioned the choice of this myth will, in all likelihood, never be known, but the appearance of the story in opera can be traced back at least to Francesco Cavalli's first Venetian opera, *Le nozze di Teti e di Peleo* (libretto by Orazio Persiani), which was produced during 1639. A discussion of Persiani's use of this episode can be found in Elizabeth Kady, "Francesco Cavalli: *Le Nozze di Teti, e di Peleo*" (master's thesis, Harvard University, 1967), pp. 34 and 80. The episode was also used in Renaissance entertainments, though it is notably absent from the long line of Florentine *intermedi*, since the Medici balked at having *Discordia* personified on their stage.

3. This translation, by Gilbert Murray, appears in William S. Fox, *The Mythology of all Races in Thirteen Volumes* (New York: Cooper Square Publishers, 1964), I:124-125.

4. From the dramatic point of view, Sbarra's decision to commence with an infernal scene makes immediately clear the fact that stage machinery will play an important role in the subsequent drama.

5. According to classical mythology Paris had a wife, whom he had deserted, called Œnone. Sbarra may have been vaguely influenced by this in his choice of the name Ennone, though his use of her in the plot bears no relationship to the myth.

6. Students of Greek mythology are well aware that the "Judgment of Paris" led more or less directly to the Trojan war; but this would have been a no more fitting conclusion for a wedding piece than Striggio's original ending for Monteverdi's *Orfeo*.

Plate I. "Ha la forza dell'oro ogni virtù": Modena, Biblioteca Estense, Ms. Mus. E. 120, fol. 31ᵛ.
(Courtesy, Biblioteca Estense)

Plate II. "Amante disprezzata": Modena, Biblioteca Estense, Ms. Mus. E. 120, fol. 68ʳ.
This is one of four pieces contained in I:MOe that are ascribed to Leopold I.
(Courtesy, Biblioteca Estense)

IL POMO D'ORO
(Music from Acts III and V
from Modena, Biblioteca Estense, Ms. Mus. E. 120)

Table of Musical Numbers

Atto Terzo

ATTO TERZO

Scena prima
Caverna d'Eolo
Eolo, Euro, Austro, Zeffiro, Volturno

Eolo
    O miei spirti che talora
quando fuora
da questi antri al mondo uscite
con soavi e dolci sibili
e con fremiti terribili
del mio nome il tutto empite,
dite, dite
quel che festi.
Vostri gesti
Sol quant'odo
del mio scettro io lieto godo.

Austro
Io dell'Affrica figlio,
che in un soffio disfaccio
del canuto Appennin l'antico ghiaccio,
a preghiere d'Amore
per distrugger nel core
della figlia d'Acrisio
un indurato inverno
che credevasi eterno
fin dagl'eterei campi
gl'ho vibrati nel seno accesi lampi,
e sempre l'ho trovata
nel suo gelo ostinata.
Ma a pena un aureo nembo
le diluviò nel grembo
che si videro a un tratto
distemprate le nevi e 'l gel disfatto.
  Così Giove trasformato
  la godé tra chiuse mura,
  ch'ove l'oro è penetrato
  mai beltà non fu sicura.
  Altre volte ei si compiacque
  di cangiarsi in cigno e in toro:
  ma la forma che sol piacque
  fu 'l disfarsi in pioggia d'oro.

[Eolo]

Ha la for- za del- l'o - ro o - gni vir - tù,   Ha la

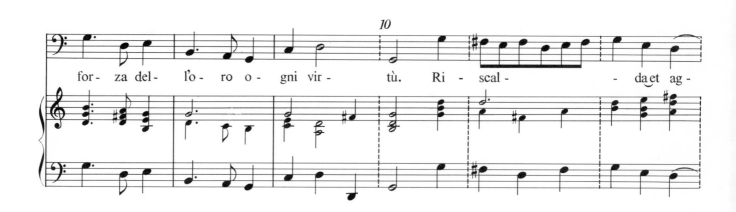

for- za del- l'o - ro o - gni vir - tù.   Ri - scal - - da et ag-

- ghiac- cia, Bo- nac- cia, Tem- pe - - sta, Tem- pe -

6

- sta Ne- gl'a- ni- mi de- sta, Ri- sve- glia, so - pi - sce, U-

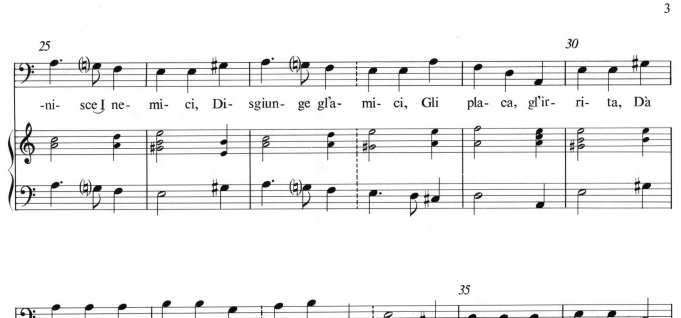

4

[Euro]

50

[1.] Un gran fa-vo- ri- to Che s'e- ra im bar- ca- to Col sof- fio bra-
2. Ei pro- vi- do e sag- gio Suo cor- so gui- da- va E ben s'au- gu-
3. Ma quan- do nel por- to Ri- dur- r'io lo vo- glio, E- gl'ur- ta in un

55

-ma- to E- stras- si dal li- to, Col sof- fio bra- ma- to E- stras- si dal li- to.
-ra- va Fe- li- ce vi- ag- gio, E ben s'au-gu- ra- va Fe- li- ce vi- ag- gio.
sco-glio E re- sta-vi ab- sor-to, E gl'ur- ta in un sco-glio E re- sta-vi ab- sor- to.

Eolo   Sian pur di questo mar l'onde tranquille,
       alle lusinghe sue non presto fede,
       ch'ove trovar il porto altri si crede
       s'incontrano talor Cariddi e Scille.

Volturno   Io spesi il mio fiato
       in certo pallone
       ch'avendo ambizione
       nell'esser gonfiato,
       alzato
       di salto,
       si vide sopra tutti ergersi in alto.
       Ma cadde, e in cadere
       si ruppe e fu aperto,
       e vòto di merto
       si fece vedere,
       e avere
       sol pieno
       di vanissimo vento il gonfio seno.

Eolo   Di fortuna il gioco è tale
       onde scherza a suo volere,
       mentre il misero mortale
       alza e abbassa per piacere
       che per farne sol cadere
       non solleva no, ma sbalza
       quei che privi di merto a un tratto inalza.

[Zeffiro]

[1.] Ed io Zef-fi - ro con Flo - ra___ Col - ti - vai con ma - ni ac-
2. Que-sti fior si___ son nu - tri - ti___ Con af - fet - to e fé sin-
3. E di que - sto___ la ca - gio - ne___ So ben io don-de de -

-cor - te Il giar - di - no___ del - la___ cor - te, Che di spe-me___ sol s'in -
-ce - ra, Ma se ben di___ pri-ma - ve - ra Son ca - du-ti il___ lan - gui -
-ri - va: Dal man-car-li___ chi l'av - vi - va, Ch'è la gra-zia___ del pa -

-fio - ra, Il giar - di - no___ del - la cor - te, Che di spe-me___
-di - ti, Ma se ben di___ pri-ma - ve - ra, Son ca - du-ti il -
-dro - ne, Dal man-car-li___ chi l'av - vi - va, Ch'è la gra-zie___

sol s'in - fio - ra, Che di spe-me___ sol s'in - fio - ra.
lan - gui - di - ti, Son ca - du-ti il___ lan - gui - di - ti.
del pa - dro - ne, Ch'è la gra - zia___ del pa - dro - ne.

SCENA SECONDA

Giunone sopra una nube, Eolo, coro di Venti

Eolo	Ma come qui Giunone
	comparisce improvisa?
Giunone	Alta cagione,
	o monarca de' venti, a te mi chiama.
Eolo	E che da te si brama?
Giunone	Sturbar un attentato il più perverso
	ed il più scelerato
	che s'udisse giamai.
Eolo	Nuovo gigante
	muover forse vuol guerra al gran tonante?
Giunone	Più temeraria impresa
	è quella ch'ha intrapresa un vil pastore.
Eolo	E che sento? e chi fu?
Giunone	Paride.
Eolo	Quel sí giusto?
Giunone	Oggi non più,
	ma sacrilego ingiusto,
	spergiuro ed infedele,
	con temerarie vele
	per rapir s'incamina
	a Sparta la regina,
	a Menelao la sposa, a noi l'onore,
	chè pur a Giove nostro Elena è figlia;
	e già sul curvo abete
	per la campagna ondosa il traditore
	intrapreso ha il viaggio,
	senza temer dell'ire
	del sovrano tonante
	per così grave oltraggio.
Eolo	O grand'ardire!

Giunone • Tu ripara agli scherni
d'una beltà rapita,
d'una reggia tradita,
d'un re sí vilipeso,
del cielo tanto offeso,
d'un ospizio violato
con termine sí indegno,
e di Giove a tal segno
dai mortali sprezzato.
     Sú sú, co' tuoi venti
frementi
ne desta
sí fiera tempesta
che il legno
disperso,
sommerso
l'indegno,
sepolti con lui
restino i falli suoi, l'offese altrui.

Eolo Diva, troppo tenuto
sono alla tua clemenza.
So che poco temuto
sarebbe il mio potere
se in quest'antri ristretto
s'avesse a contenere,
che solo è tua mercé, non già mio merto,
che me ne renda degno
poterlo esercitar nel tuo gran regno.
Di quanto imposto m'hai
ubidita sarai.

Giunone   Così confido.
Eolo Ed io così prometto.
Giunone Starò in cielo attendendo
delle promesse tue d'udir l'effetto.

Eolo   Sú sú, furie
della Terra,
non tardate,
vendicate
tant'ingiurie
con portare
oggi al Mare
orrida guerra.
Sú sú, furie
della Terra.

Coro di Venti   Là tutto
rivolgasi
il nostro potere,
il flutto
sconvolgasi
in forme sí fiere
che Paride absorto
si veda sepellir prima che morto.
          I Venti si partono a volo.

8

[SCENA TERZA]
[Valle col fiume Xanto che vi scorre per mezzo]
[Ennone sola]

[Ennone]   Ho scorsi e piani e monti
e valli e boschi e fonti,
né mai fin qui trovato
ho l'amato
mio bene.
Alle paterne arene
ora rivolgo il piè
sol per veder se forse
ei vi venisse, oh dio,
ricercando di me.
Ma folle, che dich'io?
e in sí vana credenza
ancor io mi lusingo?
e qual Paride bramo io me lo fingo?

Scena quarta

Ennone, Aurindo

Aurindo	Ma come così afflitta
	la mia bella crudele?
	Vo' in disparte sentir le sue querele.
Ennone	Geloso
	timore,
	deh lascia il mio core:
	suo dolce riposo
	deh non li sturbare.
	Ahimè, che scacciare,
	no no,
	non si può
	pensiero affannoso.
	Geloso
	timore,
	deh lascia il mio core.
	Ah, non è più quel tempo
	che solo a me rivolto
	era ogni tuo pensier, Paride mio.
	Non è più questo volto
	agl'occhi tuoi sí grato.
	L'averti troppo amato
	mi rende a te sprezzabile.
	O sorte miserabile,
	e questa è la mercede
	del mio sincero amor?
Aurindo	Così richiede
	la giustizia del cielo.
Ennone	E che fec'io?
Aurindo	Disprezzi chi t'adora,
	ed è ben giusto ancora
	che nell'istesse forme
	ricevi del tuo affetto
	a quel che ad altri dai cambio conforme.
Ennone	È troppa crudeltà
	l'aggiunger nuova pena
	a chi penando sta. Pur troppo sai
	quanto mi sian moleste
	queste importune tue vane richieste.
Aurindo	Ogni supplica mia pur troppo io so
	che a te sempre è molesta ed importuna
	e per me sempre vana,
	e che sperar fortuna
	io non posso da te bella inumana,
	poiché a guisa dell'ombra,
	se ben un sol tu sei
	che m'abbrucia e mi strugge,
	tu fuggi chi ti segue
	per seguir chi ti fugge.
Ennone	O mi fugga o mi segua,
	o m'ami o mi disprezzi,
	o che m'usi rigore
	o che m'abbia pietà,
	il bell'idolo mio
	sempre da questo core
	adorato sarà. Réstati, addio.

10

Aurindo

Addio? che conforto!
Non posso che morto
restar senza te.
Dell'anima privo
sai ben che più vivo
Aurindo non è.

[Aurindo]

En - no-ne di -spie-ta-ta, Ben veg-gio che d'un fiu - me Sol per mio mal sei

na - ta, Che da' suoi fred-di u - mo-ri hai trat-to il san - gue Per

me ge-li-do sem - pre, E del-le du-re tem-pre De-gl'al-pe - stri suoi sas - si

Ti fu l'al - ma ve - sti - ta Per me sem-pre im-pe - tri - ta.

O ca-ro Xan-to, Se gra-di-sti già ma - i Quel tri-bu-to di

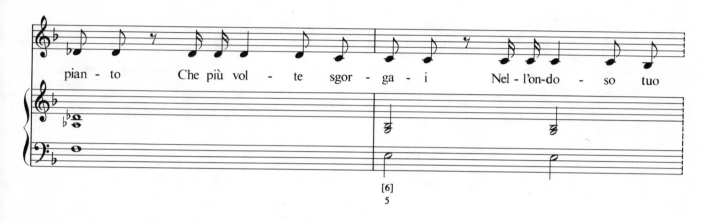

pian - to Che più vol - te sgor-ga - i Nel - l'on-do - so tuo

[6]
5

grem-bo in duo gran fiu-mi Da que-sti af-flit-ti lu - mi, Poi-ché di me pie-

-tà_____ La tua fi - glia non ha, per-met-ti al - me - no Ch'io la

7 [♮]6

12

pos - sa tro - va - re Nel tuo pro-fon-do se - - no, Che se vi-ver con le - i

Per mio cru - do de - sti - no io non po-te - i, Col mo - rir in que -

-st'ac - que Go - drò d'es - ser se - pol - to o - v'el - la nac - que. Tu

pren - di il cor - po mi - o, Ch'a lei lo spir - to in - vi - o.

SCENA QUINTA

Momo, Aurindo

Momo	Ferma, che fai?
	Se ti getti laggiù t'affogherai.
Aurindo	Posso trovar qui solo
	il rimedio al mio duolo.
Momo	T'inganni (io te lo dico
	da buono e vero amico): e che pretendi
	di trovar in un fiume?
	e che speri cavarne?
	Egli non ha che pesce,
	e l'appetito tuo non vuol che carne.
Aurindo	Tu scherzi, e pur da scherzo
	il mio male non è.
Momo	Ben te lo credo,
	Ma il rimedio non vedo
	vi si possa trovar con l'annegarsi;
	non convien disperarsi.
Aurindo	È ben finire
	con la vita il martire
	allor ch'in altro modo
	non si può terminar.
Momo	Questo non lodo.
	Tu sai che il viver nostro
	è giusto una comedia, in cui la parte
	o di servo o di re
	ch'assegnata se gl'è si rappresenta
	da ciascuno che vive.
	Questo mondo è la scena,
	che in varie prospettive ed apparati
	di sí diversi stati
	al girar d'una rota
	la volubile dea cangia in un tratto.
	Ma dopo l'ultim'atto in van s'attende
	dell'umane vicende
	altra nuova apparenza,
	perché quando la favola è finita
	restano spenti i lumi
	della speme non men che della vita,
	onde quel darsi morte è un renunziare
	a tutte le speranze.
Aurindo	E che posso sperare?
Momo	Che si cangi la scena,
	e ch'Ennone sdegnosa
	ti si renda amorosa.
Aurindo	È impossibil.
Momo	Perché?
Aurindo	Perché il suo core
	da Paride occupato
	non ammette altro amore.
Momo	Paride se n'è andato.
Aurindo	E dove è gito?
Momo	A pescar a reine in altro lito.
Aurindo	Ed Ennone?
Momo	La lascia a chi la vuole.
Aurindo	È vero?
Momo	Più che vero.
Aurindo	Or sí che non dispero.

Momo Aria

L'es - ser vi - vo a quan-to gio - va! Que-st'è l'u - ni - co con - for-to.

Se tu fos-si a - des - so mor - to Non a - vre - sti sí gran

nuo-va Da po-ter-ti con-so-la - re, E pe - rò, ⟨e pe - rò⟩ con-

-vien cam-pa - re, con-vien cam - pa - re, cam - pa - re.

[Se ne va]

te? –   Spe - ran - ze, che di - te? che,   che____ di - te?
te? –   Spe - ran - ze, che di - te? che,   che____ di - te?

[7   #6]   Ritornello
      4
      3

3. Spe - ran - ze, che di - te? che,   che____ di - te?

[7   #6]   #

E cre - der pos - s'i - o Che l'i - do - lo mi - o Si ren -

- - - da più____ mi - te?____

Spe - ran - ze, che di - te? che, che___ di - te?

7 [#]6

Spe - ran - ze, che di - te? che, che___ di - te?

[#]

[7 #6]

Ritornello

SCENA SESTA
Arsenal di Marte

Venere, Marte che sopragiunge

Venere

Questa pur è di Marte
la bellicosa sede?
E pur ei non si vede? ed in qual parte
per richieder di lui devo portarmi,
se no'l trovo né meno in mezzo all'armi?

Venere

5

[l.] Ei, for - se sa - rà, Ei, for - se sa - rà Tra vez - zi___ gio -

-co - si, Tra scher - zi a - mo - ro - si Con al - tra bel - tà?_____

Tra vez - zi__ gio - co - si, Tra scher - zi a - mo -

-ro - si Con al - tra bel - tà?_____

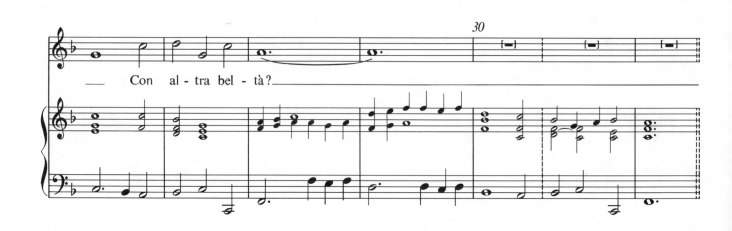

Con al - tra bel - tà?_____

Sí lie-ve, no no.

Marte	Ecco, o bella, che se n' viene
	il mio foco alla sua fera,
	che trovar ogni suo bene
	fuor ch'in te giamai non spera.
Venere	Col mio venir noioso
	forse avrò disturbato
	in qualche seno amato
	il tuo dolce riposo?
Marte	Un simil concetto
	hai dunque di me?
	E come, e perché
	sí falso sospetto?
Venere	Tue gioie impedire
	non voglio, no no.
	Tu resta, io me n' vo,
	attendi a gioire.
Marte	Gioir questo core
	per altra beltà?
	Se ciò mai sarà
	può dirtelo Amore.
Venere	D'Amor non mi fido,
	ch'ei teco s'uní
	allor che tradí
	la diva di Gnido.
Marte	E come, o mia vita,
	tradita
	ti chiami?
Venere	Perché più non vedo
	né credo
	che m'ami.
Marte	Che fede maggiore
	d'amore tu chiedi?
	Se prove già tante
	d'amante
	ti diedi?
	Il sole che l'opre
	discopre
	del mondo
	dirà s'altro affetto
	nel petto
	nascondo.
	Veder senza velo
	al cielo
	ne fe'
	che il ciel mio sereno
	tuo seno
	sol'è.

Questo sol può bearmi:
ove sotto al tuo piè deposte l'armi,
resi i trionfi miei,
amorosi trofei di tua bellezza,
maggior d'ogni grandezza,
maggior d'ogni vittoria
l'esser vinto da te stimo mia gloria.

Venere   Ed io sopra ogni diva
posso a ragion vantarmi,
se reciproco affetto
per me t'infiamma il petto, o dio dell'armi,
e 'l tuo chiaro valore
non mi lascia temere
di Pallade lo sdegno,
se ben a suo favore
arma d'Atene il re tutto il suo regno.

Marte   Cecrope, e che pretende?

Venere   Di sostenere il torto
di quest'emula mia. Distrutto e morto
vuol il frigio garzon, perché da lui
mi venne destinato
il controverso pomo.

Marte   A te fu dato
perché sol si dovea
il titol di più bella a Citerea.
Così contro 'l superbo
di Pallade campione,
in singolar tenzone
o di tanti per parte,
s'offron di sostener l'armi di Marte.

Venere   Resti da te depresso
l'orgoglio di costei
che ribelle si rende al cielo istesso
mentre che armata a contradir si muove
ai decreti di Giove.

Marte   Il giudizio di Paride fu giusto
quanto iniquo ed ingiusto
è di Pallade il senso
che sdegnata ne tiene.
Sopra questa querela
sulle libere arene
ad uso destinate
di pugne concertate
pronto a pugnar son io.
Sí gran disfida
ecco a Cecrope invio.
                 Si parte.

Venere   Sí sí, vanne, mio caro,
e sostenuta sia
nella giustizia altrui la gloria mia.

22

Venere

[1.] Trop - - po Pal - - - la-de pre - ten -
[2. Ah,_____ que-st'o - - ro quan-to lu -

- de, Se si cre-de og-gi col-l'ar - -
- ce, Gl'oc-chi ab-ba-glia e'l tut-to sfor - -

- mi L'au-reo po-mo d'u-sur-par - -
- za, On-de in ma-no del - la for - -

- mi Trop -
- za La_____

- po il giu-sto e Gio-ve of-fen - de, Trop - po il giu-sto e
____ giu-sti-zia si ri - du - ce, La_____ giu-sti-zia si

Gio - ve of - fen - de.
ri - du - ce.
Trop - po Pal -
Ah,_____ que-st'o -

la-de pre-ten - - - de.
ro quan-to lu - - - ce.]

SCENA SETTIMA

Mare

Paride, coro di suoi servi in un vascello

Coro	Alla reggia di Sparta, al soglio, al trono.
	Di Paride sono
	i regni
	sol degni,
	si lascin le selve
	di belve
	ricetti,
	più nobili affetti
	il ciel ti destina.
	Già bella regina
	del cor ti fa un dono.
	Alla reggia di Sparta, al soglio, al trono.
	Si turba il mare.
Paride	Ma come in un momento
	dibattuto e sconvolto
	quest'ondoso elemento
	cangia il tranquillo volto e lusinghiero
	in aspetto sí fiero?
1. del coro	Già sorgono in alto
	quest'atre procelle,
	e par ch'alle stelle
	minaccin l'assalto.
	Segue fiera tempesta di mare.

2. del coro	Dal vento crudele siam troppo percossi, son l'alberi scossi, squarciate le vele.
Coro	O perfidi venti, o fati malvagi, portar i naufragi in mezzo ai contenti.
3. del coro	Già vedomi absorto dai flutti perversi.
4. del coro	Già siamo sommersi.
5. del coro	Ohimè che son morto.
Coro	O perfidi venti *etc*.
Paride	Bella madre d'Amor, figlia del mare, e come puoi lasciare che là dove nascesti un tuo fido e devoto estinto resti? Dell'averti servita è questa la mercede?

Scena ottava

Paride e suo coro, Venere sopra una conchiglia
con un coro di Nereidi, Nettuno che sopra
giunge sorgendo dal mare, coro di tritoni

Venere	Eccomi pronta a prò di chi mi diede la sentenza gradita. O Nettuno, o Nettuno!
Nettuno	E che si chiede? Che orribil tempesta è questa ch'io sento? chi tal ardimento aver mai potè? chi l'ordin ne diè?
Venere	Dell'aria la regina, oggi a torto sdegnata contro Paride il giusto, coi venti congiurata per toglierli la vita turba tutta e confonde la monarchia dell'onde. Abbi di lui pietà, porgigli aita, che in premio ti prometto render a te soggetto della vaga Anfitrite tua nemica adorata il duro core.
Nettuno	Bella madre d'Amore, non men per sostenere dell'umido mio regno il diritto sovran che per godere di tue promesse il desiato effetto, con scoter il tridente che fa l'acqua e la terra in un tremare do bando alle tempeste e pace al mare. *Il mare si tranquilla.*

1. 2. del coro   Ecco quiete,
placide l'onde
del curvo abete
baciar le sponde.

3. 4. del coro   Aura fedele
in ciel sereno
di nostre vele
già gonfia il seno.

Paride   Diva d'Amore,
ondoso dio,
vostro favore
è il viver mio.

          Per voi tal calma
solo ne viene,
a voi quest'alma
deve ogni bene.

Paride e coro   Ond'è che a voi
il cor devoto
gl'affetti suoi
consacra in voto.

                    Paride parte co' suoi.

o-pra di pie-ta,＿＿＿＿＿＿＿＿＿＿ Per o-pra di pie-tà,＿＿＿＿

＿＿＿＿＿＿＿ Pre -   - mio d'A-mo -   re, P[er]

o-pra di pie-tà,＿＿＿＿＿ Per o-pra di pie-tà＿＿＿＿＿＿＿＿ Pre -

- - mio d'A-mo -   re.

[Venere parte.]

Nettuno	Non temo, no no, restar ingannato, in breve io godrò quel ricco tesoro, quella ninfa che adoro. O me beato! Il fin si darà al nostro tormento, l'amata beltà per cui mi disfaccio devo accoglier in braccio. Oh che contento!

SCENA NONA

Filaura sola

Filaura	Ove sarà sparito questo regio pastor, che non si trova chi ne sappia dar nuova? Per mar non è partito, poiché tutti dell'onde furiosi i cavalli non volevan pur ora, non che il fren del timone o de' remi lo sprone, né men del curvo abete sovra 'l dorso soffrir l'usata sella. Che terribil procella! Io che la vidi benché lunge da' lidi dal suo sdegno sicura m'ebbi quasi a svenir della paura. E questa tempesta ch'è sempre infelice dal mondo si dice fortuna di mare. E pur si dovria più tosto chiamare sventura ben ria.

SCENA DECIMA

Aurindo, Filaura

Aurindo	O Filaura!
Filaura	Che nuova?
Aurindo	Paride non si trova, e, per quello che sento, ad altri amori intento già per mar se n'è andato.
Filaura	Paride a questo tempo so che non è imbarcato, e tu per tale avviso imbarcar non ti dei nello sdruscito legno delle speranze tue.

28

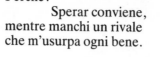

Aurindo   Gl'affetti miei
non s'imbarcano male.
Filaura   Perché?
Aurindo   Sperar conviene,
mentre manchi un rivale
che m'usurpa ogni bene.

Filaura

Quan-d'En-no-ne an-co-ra   In quei che l'a - do - ra   Non tro-vi più

fé,   Non man-ca-no a-man-ti   Fe - de-lie co - stan - ti, Fe -

-de-lie co-stan -   - ti Più de-gni di te,

Non man-ca-no a - man-ti Fe - de - lie co - stan-ti, Fe - de - lie co - stan -

- te Più de-gni di te.

Aurindo

Io pur in ser-vi-re... ...Il me - ri-to ac-

Filaura

Ma sem - pre mal vi - sto...

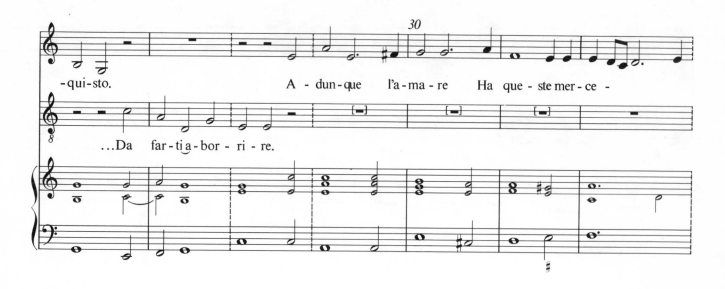

-qui-sto. A - dun-que l'a-ma - re Ha que - ste mer - ce -

...Da far - ti a - bor - ri - re.

-di? Al men, ch'è pur

Sei fol - le se cre - di For - tu - na in - con - tra - re.

po - co, Pie - to - so, pie - to - so un af - fet - to.

Di già te l'ho

Sí cru-da fie - rez-za Con va - go sem-
det - to, Per te non v'ha lo - co.

-bian - te?   Son ric - co di fe - de, Se
Un po - ve-ro a-man-te Da tut - te si sprez-za.

po - ve-ro d'o - ro.   Gl'ef-
È que-sto un te - so-ro Che mai non si ve - de.

-fet - ti vi so - no, Ben vi-sti e sti - ma - ti.

Se ven-gon por - ta - ti Con no - bi - le

E a que-sto con - sen - te A - mo - re, ch'è un nu-me?

do - no.

È ta - le il co-

O se - co-lo im-mon-do, O pes-si-mi a-

-stu - me Del se - col cor - ren - te.

-bu - si!

Vuoi for - se tu gl'u - si Cor-reg-ger del mon - do? Non gio - van la-

-men - ti, Que-re - le, né pian - ti. Chi è sen - za con-tan-ti Non

spe - ri, no no, non spe - ri con-ten - ti. Chi è sen - za con-

34

-mè son tut-te fo - le,___ Poi-ché so - le Le mo - ne-te han - no___ po-
no-me quel che bra - ma.___ E chi l'a-ma Sen - za questo in van pre-

-te - re Di ri - dur l'al - me più fie - re Ad u-sar, ad u-sar qual-
-ten - de, Che se pro-di - go non spen-de Mai pie - tà, mai pie-tà [per]___

- che mercé.   Sei sem-pli-ce, af - fé,   Se cre-di che un co - re S'ar-
___ lui non v'è.

-ren - da, S'ac - cen-da D'a - mo - re Per te.   Sei sem - pli-ce, af-

-fé, ⟨Sei sem - pli-ce, af - fé,⟩

riso

Sei sem - pli-ce, af - fé... e e e e.

SCENA UNDECIMA

Anfiteatro

Cecrope, coro de' suoi soldati

Cecrope	Ecco il campo
	ove in breve di trovarmi
	col gran Marte avrò l'onore.
	Fate al lampo
	di quest'armi
	apparir vostro valore.
	Le contese
	che s'incontran più dubbiose
	il trionfo fan più grande,
	tra l'imprese
	generose
	queste son più memorande.
Coro	Benché Marte, il dio guerriero,
	sia sí fiero,
	non però temer ne dei.
	Rendon l'armi tutti eguali,
	nostra spada anche agli dei
	saprà dar colpi mortali.

Scena duodecima

Cecrope, coro de' suoi, Marte, coro de' suoi

Cecrope	Ed ecco Marte in minacciosa fronte,
	che prima di pugnar pensa fugarmi.
	Sú, miei fedeli, a vendicar con l'armi
	dell'adirata dea gl'oltraggi e l'onte.
Marte	Tanto ardito un uom mortale
	contro me venir presume?
	Per combatter contro un nume
	tuo potere è troppo frale.
Cecrope	Vengo, o Marte, ove mi chiami,
	ubidisco ai cenni tuoi,
	s'io ti servo in quel che vuoi,
	e che più da me tu brami?
Marte	In che forza sperar puoi?
Cecrope	In quel giusto ch'io difendo.
Marte	La giustizia è sol per noi.
Cecrope	Ch'è per me provarti intendo.
a 2	Non si sfoghin le nostr'ire
	in contrasti di parole,
	sú sú, all'arme, in cui si suole
	la ragion far apparire.

*Segue abbattimento tra Marte
e li suoi seguaci e Cecrope
e li suoi soldati con la
peggior di questi, che
restano prigionieri di Marte.*

Marte	Cedi, che vinto sei.
Cecrope	Così vuole il mio fato.
Marte	Anzi, quel dritto
	ch'io sostengo e difendo.
Cecrope	Alla fortuna tua cedo e m'arrendo.
a 2	Della pugna l'onore

della sorte $\left\{\begin{array}{l}\text{non è, ma}\\\text{sol'è, non}\end{array}\right\}$ del valore.

[ATTO QUINTO]

[SCENA PRIMA]

[Villa deliziosa di Paride]

[Ennone]

[*Ennone*]

[1.] O Pa - ri-de a - ma - to, Che lun - ghe di - mo - re Da me slon - ta -
[2. Pur que-sto è il sog - gior - no Del - l'i - do - lo mi - o, Ne me - no qui in-

-na - to Per tan-te e tan - t'o - re, Da me slon - ta - na - to Per
-tor - no Ve - der - lo pos - s'i - o, Né me - no qui in - tor - no Ve-

tan-te e tan - t'o - re Io son tut-t'ar - do - re, Né ar - ri-vo in che
-der - lo pos - s'i - o, Né in - ten - der, oh di - o, Pur do - ve si

lo-co Mio fo-co Si stà,] E do-ve sa - rà? Ohi - mè, ⟨Ohi-
tro-va Chi nuo-va Ne dà,] }

-mè,⟩ Non so che Di me-sto e in-fe - li - ce_____ A que - st'al-ma do - len-te il

cor pre - di - ce, A que - st'al-ma do - len-te il

cor pre - di - ce.

SCENA SECONDA

Filaura, Ennone, Momo

Filaura	O figlia, o figlia mia!
Ennone	E che porti, o nutrice?
Filaura	Novella la più ria
	che ti possa arrivar. Già s'è imbarcato
	il tuo Paride amato.
Ennone	Come? quando? perché?
Momo	Per quello che poc' anzi
	(ma a tempo) io v'avvisai,
	e voi non lo credeste,
	perché a quei che si vede
	sotto povera veste
	non si dà molta fede.
Ennone	Dunque è ver che mi sprezzi,
	mi fugga e m'abandoni?
	dove, dove, dov'è?
	Voglio che senta almeno
	i rimproveri miei.
Filaura	Deh, ferma il piè,
	ch'a tempo più non sei.
Ennone	Dunque è partito?
Momo	È dal lido sparito in un momento,
	che lo portava il vento.
Ennone	Così tradisce, ahimè,
	il mio amor, la mia fé?

42

-tà, Ri - vol - gi - ti in qua, Se a pie - no con - ten - ta Vuoi pur che si
può. Tu bra - mi, ch'io 'l so. Tuo cru - do de - si - re Ve - der - mi mo -

sen - ta La tua cru - del - tà. Ma l'a - ni - ma stan - ca Nel
-ri - re Al - tro - ve non può.

lun - go tor - men - to Già sen - to Che man - ca, Già

sen - to Che man - ca. O mor - te so - a - ve, In

44

Filaura Ohimè che s'è svenuta!
Momo 　　　　　　　O meschinella.
Filaura Presto, Momo, m'aiuta.
Momo Son pronto. Oh, com'è bella!
Filaura Andiamola a spruzzare
　　　　　alla fonte vicina.
Momo Per farla ritornare
　　　　　saria meglio condurla a una cantina.

SCENA TERZA

Giunone in una nube oscurissima, Giove
sopra l'aquila che sopragiunge

Giunone   E ancor invendicata
per l'eterea campagna
Giunon tant'oltraggiata in van si lagna?

46

Giove   Tempra gli sdegni omai,
             e dell'arbitro d'Ida
             t'acquieta alla sentenza.
Giunone   È troppo ingiusta.
Giove   A che tanta doglienza
             sol per un pomo d'oro?
             mentre tutto possiedi
             dell'empirea magion l'ampio tesoro?

-rà?   Que - sto poi no, Gia - mai non   sof - fri-

-rò, no no no,   Que - sto poi no, Gia - mai non   sof - fri - rò.

Giove	Abbia pur la pretenzione
	d'una simil vanità
	chi non ha
	né può aver altr'ambizione;
	ma, Giunone,
	altri vanti aver ben dei,
	mentre mia suora e mia consorte sei.
Giunone	Fra le dive più sublimi
	ben lo vedo
	ch'io possedo
	sú nel cielo i posti primi;
	ma che vale,
	se rimessa
	son io stessa
	all'arbitrio di un mortale?
Giove	Ei da me fu deputato.
Giunone	Senza questo ei non ardiva.
Giove	A mio nome ha giudicato.
Giunone	L'ingiustizia a te s'ascriva.

[*Giunone*]

[1.] Giu - di - car   ret - - to e sin - ce - ro

2. È d'un gran - - de un   gran-d'er - ro - re

Tu do - ve - vi fra gli__ de - i,
Il ri - met - ter si ad__ al - tru - i

Né sgra - var - ti del__ pen - sie - ro__
D'un af - fa - re ch'è il__ mag - gio - re__

E del - l'o - bli - go in__ che__ se - i,
Pos - sa a - ver ne' re - gni su - i,

Né sgra - var - ti del___ pen - sie - ro__ E del-
D'un af - fa - re ch'è il__ mag - gio - re__ Pos - sa a-

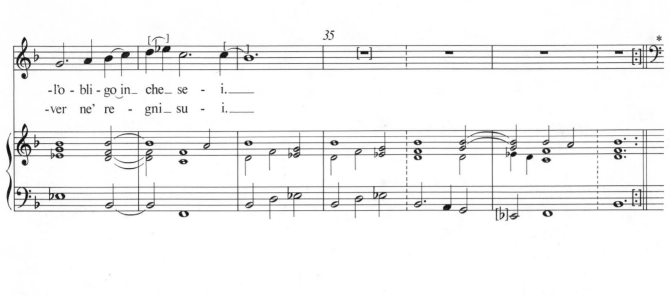

-l'o - bli - go in che se i._____
-ver ne' re - gni su - i._____

Giove

Quan - do ve - drò ces - sa - re Nel tuo tur - ba - to sen sí gran tem - pe - sta

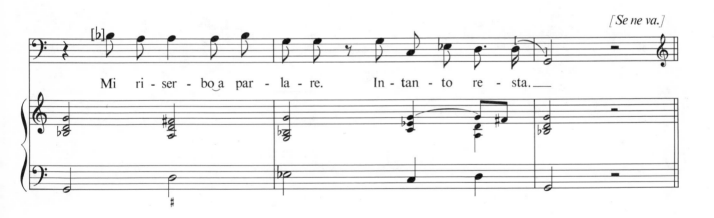

[Se ne va.]

Mi ri - ser - bo a par - la - re. In - tan - to re - sta._____

Giunone

Van - ne pur, che se Gio - ve Og - gi per me non se - i Po - co gra - to ri-

50

-e - sci a - gl'oc - chi_ mie - i. Ma già ch'in ciel né in

ter - ra La giu - sti - zia p⟨er⟩ me non ha più lo - co, Poi - ché l'ac - qua_ed il

fo - co Nie - gan an - che di far le mie ven - det - te, Vo' ne l'e - te - re - o re - gno

Ol - trag - gia - ta dei - tà sfo - gar_____ lo_____ sde - gno.__

D'un or-ri-do ve-lo, ⟨D'un or-ri-do ve-lo⟩__ L'a - ria s'in-gom - - - - - bre,__ Di nu-bi e d'om - bre__ Co - - - - pra-si il cie - lo,

[S'annuvola.]

[Ritornello?]

E'l nu-me di De-lo I rag - - - gi più pu - ri O-

52

[Scena quarta]

[Momo, Giunone come sopra]

Momo

O - là, di - va che fa - i? Vuoi for - se tem - pe - star? A -

-dun-que tu non sa - i La tua rab - bia sfo-gar in al - tra gui - sa? Che gran ven-

-det - ta, ah ah, ah ah, scop - pio di ri - sa!

Giunone

Del - l'a - ria nei cam-pi, ⟨Del - l'a - ria nei cam-pi⟩ Già so - no in

[Si vedono

ar - - - - mi,__ A ven-di-

lampi e saette.]

-car - mi__ Tur - - bi -ni e lam - - pi.

Violi[ni]

Il cie - lo s'av - vam-pi, Si por - - ti a la

ter - ra La guer-ra, Sù pre - sti, E re - sti, E re - sti Pur tut - -

40

-to Dal tor - ri-do Ed or - - - ri-do Mio sde - -

[♯]   [♯]   [♯] [6]   [6]

50

- gno de - strut - to, Dal tor - ri-do Ed or - -

[♯]   [6]

[Comincia il temporale di pioggia e grandine.]

55   *60*

- ri - do Mio sde - - - gno de - strut - to.

Momo

[1.] Ven - ga pur fie - - ra tem - pe - sta, Che di

[♮]   7   6   [♯5] [♯]

que - sta Io non ho pun - to pa - u - ra. La mia lin - gua m'as - si -

-cu - ra,__ La mia lin - gua m'as - si - cu - ra__ Che non déi, s'in zuc-ca hai

sa - le, Stuz-zi - car - mi a dir__ del__ ma - le, Stuz-zi -

-car - mi a dir__ del__ ma - le.

[Cresce il temporale.]

Ritornello

star_____ al tuo__ di - spet - to.

Ritornello

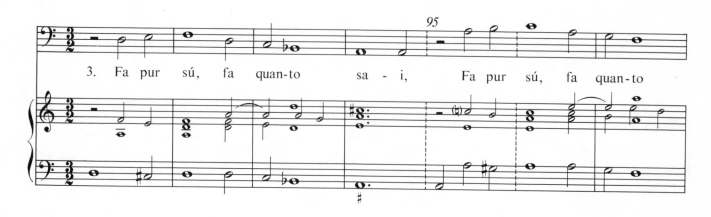

3. Fa pur sú, fa quan-to sa - i, Fa pur sú, fa quan-to

sa - i, Che già ma - i__ Non vo' to - glier - mi di qui;

Quan-do be - ne tut - to un dí Tu pio - ves - si an - che dei sas - si,

di   due   pas - si. ____

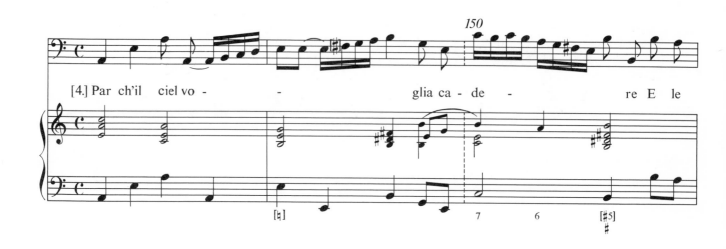

[4.] Par   ch'il   ciel   vo - - glia ca - de - re   E   le

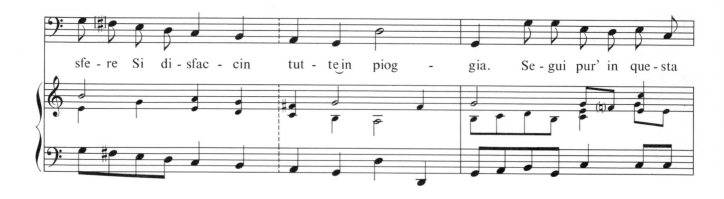

sfe - re   Si   di - sfac - cin   tut - te in   piog - gia.   Se - gui   pur' in   que - sta

fog - gia, ___   Se - gui   pur' in   que - sta   fog - gia, ___   O   Giu - no - ne, ad am - mol -

Che do-poi con lo stil mi-o Sa-prò ben _____ sciac-quar-ti an-

-ch'i - o, Sa-prò ben _____ sciac-quar-ti an - ch'i - o.

Il di - lu - vio è ces - sa - to, ed io più du-ro Di Giu-no - ne son

sta - to. Pria che ve-der-mi muo-ve-re, È con-ve-nu-to a lei re-star di pio-ve-re.

Ma quan-to, oh,_____ quan-to ma-le Ha fat-to il tem-po-ra-le: ec-co ca-du-ta Di Pa-ri-de la pe-na So-vra il suo bel sog-gior-no, ec-co ab-bat-tu-ta La sua pom-pa sí a-me-na, ec-co de-

-strut - ta O-gni de-li-zia sua più va-ga e bel-la.

E co - sì a pun - to va: Quei ch'il mo - do non ha Da

bat - ter il ca - val, bat - - - te la sel - la.

[SCENA QUINTA]

Musica di Sua M[aestà] C[esarea]

[Ennone sola]

A - man - te di - sprez-

no no no, no no no no no, Al-tra spe-me non re-sta In co-sì du-ra

sor - te Che fi - nir_ Il mar-tir,_‹Che fi - nir_ Il mar-tir›_ Con _ la mia mor -

-te, Che fi - nir_ Il mar - tir,_Che fi - nir_ Il mar - tir_ Con la mia mor - te.

[1.] Lo stra-le_ pun - gen-te Che cu - ra so - ven-te E dol - ce di -

-por-to Mi fu ne' pri-mi an-ni, Mi fu ne' pri-mi an-ni Il so-lo con-

-for-to, Il so-lo con - for-to An - ch'og-gi mi si - a, Che que - st'a - ni-ma

mi - a Le - vi_ d'af - fan - ni, Il so-lo con - for-to An-

-ch'og - gi mi si - a, Che que - st'a - ni-ma mi - a, ⟨Che que - st'a - ni-ma mi - a⟩

Le - vi __ d'af - fan __ - ni, [Le - vi __ d'af - fan __ - ni.]

2. Se già __ tra __ le __ sel - ve Fe - ri - va le bel - ve, Più cru - da è la

fie - ra Ch'an - ni - do nel pet - to, Ch'an - ni - do nel pet - to; Tra-

-fig - ga - si e pe - ra, Tra - fig - ga - si e pe - ra Con que - sto mio cor Quel-

-l'em - pio tra-di - tor,   Quel - l'em - pio tra-di - tor   Che v'ha ri - cet - to.

SCENA SESTA

Aurindo, Ennone

Aurindo	Ferma, mia vita.
Ennone	Oh dio,
	e chi nel viver mio
	mi prolunga il morire?
Aurindo	Un tuo costante
	tanto fedel quanto infelice amante.
Ennone	Lasciami questo strale.
Aurindo	Io ben lo lascerò
	quando vogli però
	il suo colpo mortale
	volger contro di me.
Ennone	Lascia, se m'ami,
	lascialo, se tu brami
	far pago il mio desire.

SCENA SETTIMA

Filaura, Ennone, Aurindo

Filaura	No no, lasciala dire,
	tienlo, Aurindo, pur forte,
	che non si dia la morte;
	sí sí, tienlo pur stretto.
	Che tu sii benedetto, oh come appunto
	a tempo sei qui giunto!
Ennone	E tu ancor, o nodrice,
	vieni d'un infelice
	a disturbar la pace?
Filaura	Anzi, darla vorrei,
	ma come tu la cerchi a me non piace.
	Già colui se n'è andato
	a cercar altri amori,
	né creder che se mori
	ei ti resti obligato.

Ennone   Io più non curo
quel perfido spergiuro,
voglio solo finire
con una breve morte
un continuo morire.
Filaura   Credimi, figlia mia,
che quanto all'ammazzarsi è una pazzia.

[Filaura] Aria

[1.] La-scia an - dar ___ chi se ne va, ___ Ed at - ten-di a quel che
2. Or pen - sar ___ più non si de ___ A quel Pa - ri-de in-co-

vie ___ ne: So che Au - rin-do ti vuol be - ne, Ed an - cor te ne ___ vor - rà, ___
-stan ___ te, Ma tro - var-si [un] al - tro a-man-te Che ti ser - bi a-mo - re e ___ fé, ___

___ Ed an - cor te ne ___ vor - rà, ___ On-de
___ Che ti ser - bi a-mo - re e ___ fé. ___ Tal Au -

Ennone   Ah Paride spietato, e ben si vede
       che da un'orsa crudel fosti allevato!

*Ennone's two lines "Ah Paride . . . fosti allevato" form an interjection
between the two strophes of Filaura's aria "Lascia andar chi se ne va."

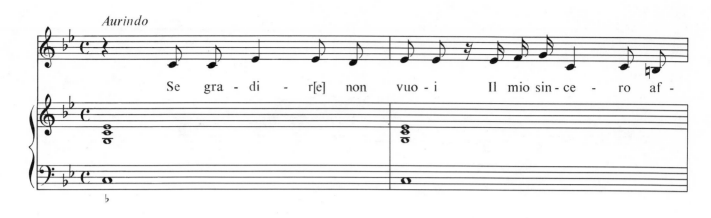

Aurindo

Se gra - di - r[e] non vuo - i Il mio sin - ce - ro af -

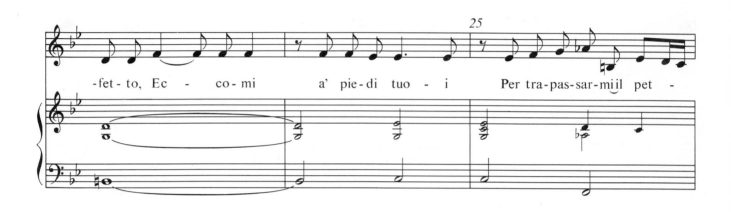

-fet - to, Ec - co - mi a' pie - di tuo - i Per tra-pas-sar-mi il pet -

- to, La sen - ten - za n'a - spet - to, ch'o di

mor - te o di vi - ta, Pur che ven - ga da te, mi fia gra - di - ta.

Ennone: Ti ce - do. M'ar - ren-do.

Aurindo: E che ve - do? Che sen - to? Au - rin - do con-

Filaura:

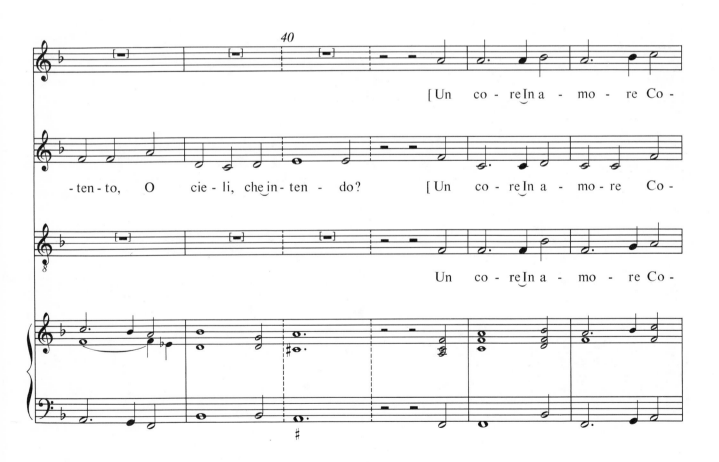

-ten - to, O cie - li, che in - ten - do? [Un co - re In a - mo - re Co-

[Un co - re In a - mo - re Co-

Un co - re In a - mo - re Co-

-stan - - te, Fe - de - le, Può ren - der-si a - man-te U -

-stan - - te, Fe - de - le, Può ren - der-si a - man-te U -

-stan - - te, Fe - de - le, Può ren - der-si a - man-te U -

-n'al - ma _ cru - de - le, Può ren - der-si a - man-te U - n'al - ma _ cru -

-n'al - ma cru - de - le, Può ren - der-si a - man-te U - n'al - ma cru -

-n'al - ma cru - de - le, Può ren - der-si a - man-te U - n'al - ma cru -

-de- le. Un co - re In a - mo - re Co - stan - - te, Fe -

-de- le. Un co - re In a - mo - re Co - stan - te, Fe -

-de- le. Un co - re In a - mo - re Co - stan - - te, Fe -

-de - le, Co - stan - - te Fe - de - le.]

-de - le, Co - stan - te Fe - de - le.]

- de - le, Co - stan - - te Fe - de - le.

SCENA OTTAVA

Momo, Ennone, Aurindo, Filaura

Momo	Buon prò vi faccia amici.
	Aurindo, ora che dici?
	e non ti sottoscrivi
	alla sentenza mia,
	che attendere si deve a star tra i vivi?
	Se dianzi t'affogavi,
	a quel che giunto sei non arrivavi.
Filaura	Dopo aver ben diluviato
	piogge il cielo e gl'occhi pianti,
	ecco al fin pur è arrivato
	il seren de' nostri amanti.
a 4	O voi che penate,
	o voi che languite,
	soffrite,
	sperate,
	che al fin la mercede
	riportano in amor costanza e fede.

SCENA NONA

Piazza del castello di Marte col suo palazzo nel prospetto e nel mezzo una torre isolata. S'apre il cielo, ove nel suo trono si vede assiso maestosamente Giove con l'aquila a' piedi, Giunone vicino a lui, Pallade ed un coro numeroso di varie deità.

Giove, Giunone, Pallade, coro di dei

Giove	E per un pomo d'oro
	di così lieve pondo
	andar dovrà tutto sossopra il mondo?
	E Pallade, ch'è parto
	della testa d'un Giove,
	per sí debol cagion tant'armi muove?
Pallade	L'ingiustizia evidente,
	oltraggiando la terra, offende il cielo,
	onde di giusto zelo
	s'armano contro lei
	non meno de' mortali anco gli dei.
Giunone	Se per zelo del giusto
	che chiede vendicarmi
	arma Pallade sol, giuste son l'armi.
Pallade	Alla giustizia intendo
	di servir ancor io,
	mentre quello ch'è mio
	a chi me l'usurpò toglier pretendo.
Giunone	Per propri interessi
	armata tu sei?
Pallade	D'Astrea son gl'istessi
	i dritti che i miei.

Giunone	Il pomo è un tributo che venne a Giunone.
Pallade	È solo dovuto a me di ragione.
Giunone	Io sono regina.
Pallade	Io Pallade armata.
Giunone	Il tutto m'inchina.
Pallade	Io sono adorata.
Giunone	Chi meco contrasta?
Pallade	Or or lo vedremo.
Giunone	Non stimo quell'asta.
Pallade	Tuo scettro non temo.
Giove	Olà, figlia e consorte, olà, che sento? Come tal ardimento del gran tonante al riverito soglio? Di sí fiera tenzon la malnata cagion sopprimer voglio.

     Giove fulmina la torre della
      fortezza, e la fa cadere.

    L'erario ecco atterrato
    del vostro sí stimato
    controverso tesoro.
    Vanne, o ministra mia,
    ritrova il pomo d'oro, e a me si dia.

      L'aquila vola dal cielo tra
      le rovine della torre.

     Quei che vuole in tempo breve
    risanar ogni gran male,
    pria che rendasi mortale
    la cagion toglier ne deve.

      Ritorna l'aquila a Giove
      col pomo nel rostro.

    Così le vostre risse
    per tanta e sí gran lite,
    emulatrici dee, saran finite.

Pallade *Giunone*	La lite finirà se l'aureo pomo a {Palla / Giunon} si darà. S'aspetta a me, d'altri certo non è.
Pallade	Padre, . . .
Giunone	germano e sposo, . . .
Pallade *Giunone*	questi son pregi miei. Fanne veder che sei giusto e {pietoso. / amoroso.}
Pallade	Son tua figlia, . . .
Giunone	Io sorella, . . .
Pallade	del tuo ciel . . .
Giunone	del tuo letto
a 2	la delizia più bella.
Pallade	Mio caro . . .
Giunone	Mio diletto . . .
Pallade	padre, . . .
Giunone	germano e sposo, . . .
Pallade *Giunone*	questi son pregi miei. Fanne veder che sei giusto e {pietoso. / amoroso.}

Scena decima
Venere sopra il suo carro salisce dalla fortezza al cielo
Giove, Giunone, Pallade, Venere, coro di dei

Venere	O cielo, ov'è la fede? e la sentenza
	che giustamente diede
	un Paride sí retto,
	che per arbitro eletto
	fu dall' alto tonante,
	or retrattar si deve?
	Così dunque di lieve ed inconstante
	(ah, stravaganze nuove)
	condanni il tuo giudizio, o sommo Giove?
Giove	Voglio rendervi tutte
	satisfatte egualmente,
	vincitrici e contente.
Giunone	E come?
Pallade	Ed in che modo?
Venere	Ed in che forma?
tutte 3	No no, Giove, no no,
	questo dar non si può.
Giove	Voglio che si riserbi
	il controverso pomo alla maggiore
	e più degna eroina
	che il grand'occhio del sole
	sia per veder già mai, consorte e prole
	de' più chiari e sublimi
	che devan sostenere
	di due gran monarchie gli scettri primi.
	In questa ammirerai
	le tue glorie, o Giunone,
	per le tante corone
	che l'ingemmano il crine. E nel suo spirto
	le tue doti divine,
	o Pallade, dal fato
	contemplar ti fia dato.
	E nella sua bellezza
	goderai di vedere,
	bella madre d'Amore,
	le tue sembianza vere.
Giunone	E in questa uniti
	si vedran tanti pregi?
Giove	A questa, che sarà d'invitti regi,
	di monarchi e d'augusti
	augustissima sposa e madre e figlia,
	sí saggia e spiritosa,
	e bella a meraviglia,
	serbando il pomo d'oro, al fine spente
	saran tante contese,
	e voi tutte contente
	d'averne conseguite
	le bramate vittorie,
	chè se le vostre glorie
	in lei saranno unite
	può ciascuna di voi
	dir che coi pregi suoi vinse la lite.

Giunone	
Pallade	E come esser potrà che mai si veda. . .
Venere	

Giunone	tal grandezza?
Pallade	tal senno?
Venere	e tal beltà?
Giove	Or tu, de' miei decreti

alata esecutrice,
conserva l'aureo pomo
a quell'età felice
in cui per fecondar d'augusti e regi
una stirpe immortale
l'aquila imperiale ai dolci rai
di sí grand'eroina arder vedrai,
ch'è sol dovuto a lei
questo premio divino.
S'apran pur del destino
ne' celesti musei gl'occulti arcani,
che d'ammirar son vago
prima dell'avvenir sí bella imago.

> *Giove ritiratosi a destra, e Giunone*
> *a sinistra, s'aprono le stanze*
> *del Fato, che dilatandosi in una*
> *gran lontananza vi si vedono*
> *l'effigie di S.[ua] M.[aestà]*
> *C.[esarea] e dell'imperatrice*
> *con numerosa prole ed all'intorno*
> *tutte l'imagini degl'imperatori,*
> *re, ed altri prencipi dell'augu-*
> *stissima Casa d'Austria.*

Giunone	E che veggio?
Pallade	E che miro?
Venere	E che stupida ammiro?
Giove	Ecco là tra l'idee

degl'AUSTRIACI regnanti
quella che deve, o emulatrici dee,
tutti nelle sue glorie
unire i vostri vanti. Oh, come godo
vederla in santo nodo
congiunta al gran LEOPOLDO
per arricchir l'Europa
de' più famosi eroi
che si pregi la fama
portar dai lidi esperii ai regni eoi!
Contemplate e stupite,
e insieme riverite
la cagione verace
che unir sola vi può con dolce pace.

Giunone	Che maestà!
Pallade	Che spirto!
Venere	E che vaghezza!
tutte 3	Magnanima eroina!

Giunone	Riverente Giunone
Pallade	Pallade ossequiosa a te s'inchina,
Venere	E Venere devota

ed il pomo ti cede,
che di te non si vede
né già mai si vedrà . . .

Giunone	di stirpe e di grandezza . . .
Venere	di grazia e di beltà . . .
Pallade	di senno e di valore . . .
tutte 3	meraviglia maggiore.
Giove e le 3 dee	Non può sott'uman velo

Giove { *Giunone* / *Pallade* / *Venere* } la più { grande / saggia / bella } di te formare il cielo.

le 3 dee	Onde non più discordi
	ma nelle glorie tue siamo concordi.
Giove	Dee ben sperar il mondo
	il tranquillo seren d'un secol d'oro
	da quei benigni lumi,
	se può l'imagin loro
	placar il cielo e concordare i numi!

Giunone / *Pallade* / *Venere* } Gioiscan dunque a questre nostre paci / de' rai di sí bel sol chiari trofei. . .

Giunone	gl'aerei spirti miei.
Pallade	di Pallade i seguaci.
Venere	e di quell'acque
	ove Venere nacque
	i più leggiadri mostri.
tutte 3	Così ai giubili nostri
	si vedran festeggiare
	l'aria, la terra e 'l mare.
Giove	Per sí lieto accidente
	come tutte contente,
	belle dive, voi sete,
	del secolo felice
	che il destin ne predice
	anche godete.
	Ecco tutto svelato
	quest'arcano del Fato,
	di sí lieti imenei
	ecco i bramati frutti.
	Ne festeggino tutti
	oggi gli dei.
1. del coro	Sí sí, giubiliamo,
	godiamo,
	è ben giusto
	che ognor più vivace
	di germi ferace
	sia l'albero AUGUSTO
	sull'Istro regnante,
	che Atlante
	più degno
	esser deve del ciel l'alto sostegno.

Venere / *Giunone* / *Pallade* / *coro di dei* } O bell'età, che da quel sen fecondo / propagata vedrà l'AUSTRIACA prole, / onde delle sue glorie al più bel sole / si rassereni il ciel, s'illustri il mondo.

Si cangia la scena inferiore in una gran piazza di ricchi e superbi edificii col mare nel prospetto, seguendo nel medesimo tempo tre balli differenti

di spiritelli in aria,
di cavalieri in terra,
di sirene e tritoni in mare.

IL FINE